POLLINATION PALS

SUPER SCIENCE

JODIE MANGOR

Rourke®

Before Reading: *Building Background Knowledge and Vocabulary*

Building background knowledge can help children process new information and build upon what they already know. Before reading a book, it is important to tap into what children already know about the topic. This will help them develop their vocabulary and increase their reading comprehension.

Questions and Activities to Build Background Knowledge:

1. Look at the front cover of the book and read the title. What do you think this book will be about?
2. What do you already know about this topic?
3. Take a book walk and skim the pages. Look at the table of contents, photographs, captions, and bold words. Did these text features give you any information or predictions about what you will read in this book?

Vocabulary: *Vocabulary Is Key to Reading Comprehension*

Use the following directions to prompt a conversation about each word.

- Read the vocabulary words.
- What comes to mind when you see each word?
- What do you think each word means?

> ### Vocabulary Words:
> - adapt
> - crops
> - dung
> - hover
> - mammals
> - nectar
> - pollinators
> - species

During Reading: *Reading for Meaning and Understanding*

To achieve deep comprehension of a book, children are encouraged to use close reading strategies. During reading, it is important to have children stop and make connections. These connections result in deeper analysis and understanding of a book.

 Close Reading a Text

During reading, have children stop and talk about the following:

- Any confusing parts
- Any unknown words
- Text to text, text to self, text to world connections
- The main idea in each chapter or heading

Encourage children to use context clues to determine the meaning of any unknown words. These strategies will help children learn to analyze the text more thoroughly as they read.

When you are finished reading this book, turn to the next-to-last page for **Text-Dependent Questions** and an **Extension Activity**.

TABLE OF CONTENTS

POLLINATORS

Do you like crunching into an apple? How about almonds? Cucumbers? If so, you can thank honeybees! Bees act as **pollinators**. They help many plants reproduce.

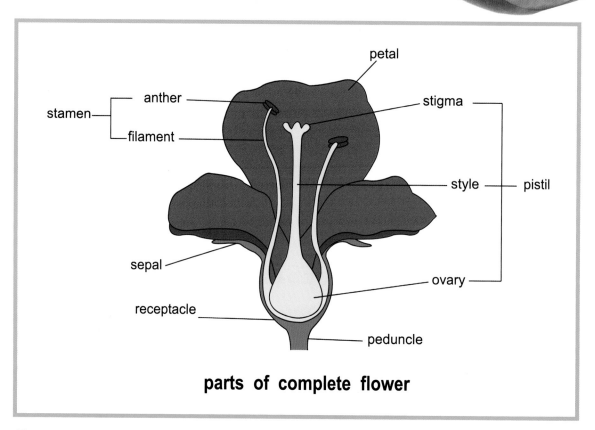

parts of complete flower

To make a seed, the female part of the plant, called a pistil, needs pollen from the male part of the flower, called a stamen.

Pollen Power!
Pollinators move pollen from a male part of a flower to a female part. Sometimes this happens inside a single flower. Sometimes the male and female parts are in different flowers.

This is how a bee gets the job done. It visits a flower and collects sticky **nectar**. Pollen from the male part of a flower sticks to the bee. The bee flies to another flower. The pollen rubs off. If the pollen lands on a female flower part, a seed can form. Sometimes a fruit, such as an apple or a cucumber, grows around the seed.

Most pollinators are insects. But birds and other animals can be pollinators too. Many plants and pollinators **adapt** to each other. A flower's color and smell are important. So are its size and shape. These things help attract certain pollinators.

Flowers of the saguaro cactus can be pollinated by bats, woodpeckers, and insects.

European peacock butterfly

Moths land on flowers that smell strong and sweet. Red flowers attract different insects than purple flowers do. Birds use their long beaks to reach into deep flowers. Pollinators are rewarded. They get sweet nectar or pollen to eat.

BEES AND OTHER BUGS

Most flowers are pollinated by insects that can fly. They can easily move from flower to flower.

Honeybees are pollination superstars. They look for yellow, blue, and purple flowers. They move a lot of pollen around. They take some nectar and pollen back to their hives. Bees turn nectar into honey. They eat the pollen. Many of the **crops** we eat depend on honeybees for pollination.

Barely a Buzz
The United States has lost more than half of its honeybee colonies. Honeybees are dying. Scientists are trying to figure out why.

Butterflies pick up less pollen than bees do. But they visit more red flowers. They can see red. Bees can't. Butterflies also like orange, yellow, pink, and blue. They visit a lot of wildflowers.

Moths are active at night. They visit white flowers that smell sweet. They drink a lot of nectar. They can carry pollen over long distances.

Both moths and butterflies need to land before feeding. They look for flowers with a landing area.

Small in Size, Big in Number
More than 200 thousand **species** of insects are pollinators. This includes flies, beetles, wasps, ants, butterflies, moths, and bees.

Flies and beetles like rotting meat and **dung**. Flowers that are pollinated by flies smell like these things. They are purple or brown. They do not make nectar, only pollen. The flies and beetles feed on the pollen.

At a Crawl
Ants are good nectar eaters, but they aren't the best pollinators. Many flowers have sticky hairs that keep ants out.

Ants love to eat nectar. But they can't fly. To get nectar, they crawl from flower to flower. They visit flowers low to the ground and close to the stem.

BIRDS AND BATS

Some birds are pollinators. Birds are attracted to large red, orange, or purple flowers. The flowers hold a lot of nectar. The pollen is very sticky. It attaches to feathers and beaks.

About 2,000 species of birds are pollinators.

Hummingbirds **hover** to drink nectar. Other birds perch. Some birds have sharp beaks and claws. Flowers pollinated by these birds must be strong.

In tropical regions, birds pollinate food crops. These include banana, papaya, and nutmeg.

Bats pollinate the flowers of more than 500 plant species. They are important to mangoes, avocados, cocoa, and others. Bats like large, white, and bell-shaped flowers. The blooms open at night. They smell strong.

Some bats have very long tongues. They can reach nectar at the bottom of flowers.

Super Stinky
Bats called flying foxes pollinate durian flowers. The durian is known as the world's smelliest fruit.

BIG POLLINATORS

Lemurs are the world's largest pollinators. Some climb traveler's trees in Madagascar. They open up a flower. Then they lick the nectar and pollen. Pollen gets onto their snouts and fur. It hitches a ride to the next flower.

Lemurs also eat fruit, leaves, seeds, bark, and sap from different types of trees.

AUSTRALIA

brushtail possum

sugar glider

flying fox

Other **mammals** are pollinators too. In South Africa, rodents pollinate sugarbush plants. The flowers smell like sour milk or cheese.

Scientists have found that lizards can be pollinators. On some islands, geckos and skinks drink nectar from flowers. Pollen sticks to their scales. It gets passed from flower to flower.

ACTIVITY

Make a Pollinator

Design an insect pollinator and flowers that it can pollinate.

Supplies

- pipe cleaners
- coffee filters
- drinking straws
- sticks
- cotton balls
- cotton swabs
- clothespins
- scissors
- tape
- glue
- two paper cups
- orange drink mix powder

Directions

1. Save the two paper cups for making flowers. Then, use any of the remaining supplies to create an insect pollinator.

2. As you design it, think about how this insect will drink nectar. How will it move pollen?

3. Next, make two flowers using the paper cups, pipe cleaners, and tape.

4. Sprinkle a small spoonful of orange drink mix powder in the bottom of the cup. This will be the pollen.

5. Fly the insect you made in and out of the flower cups.

6. Did you make a pollinator that can spread pollen from one flower to another?

Pollinators Need Protection
Insects and animals pollinate about 90 percent of the world's plants. Pollinator populations are decreasing. Shrinking habitats, pesticides, and climate change are among the causes for their decline.

GLOSSARY

adapt (uh-DAPT): to change to fit in better with the environment

crops (krahps): plants grown for food for people or animals

dung (duhng): solid waste from an animal

hover (HUHV-ur): to remain in one place in the air

mammals (MAM-uhls): warm-blooded animals that have hair or fur and usually give birth to live babies

nectar (NEK-tur): a sweet liquid produced by flowers

pollinators (PAH-luh-nate-uhrs): something, such as an insect, that carries pollen from one plant or part of a plant to another

species (SPEE-seez): groups of plants or animals whose members can mate and have offspring

INDEX

TEXT-DEPENDENT QUESTIONS

1. How do flowers and pollinators help each other?

2. Name three pollinators that are not insects.

3. What are two ways plants and their pollinators have adapted to each other?

4. Which animals pollinate at night?

5. What characteristics of a flower attract pollinators?

EXTENSION ACTIVITY

Plant a pollinator garden. If you don't have much space, you can grow the plants in containers filled with soil. Choose a variety of native flowering plants. The flowers should have different colors and shapes. The more variety there is, the more pollinators you'll attract. Do not use chemicals near your pollinator garden. Observe the flowers and their visitors.

ABOUT THE AUTHOR

Jodie Mangor writes magazine articles and books for children. She is also the author of audio tour scripts for high-profile museums and tourist destinations around the world. Many of these tours are for kids. She lives in Ithaca, New York, with her family.

© 2020 Rourke Educational Media

www.rourkebooks.com

PHOTO CREDITS: Civer, page 1: ©RebeccaBloomPhoto; page 3, 22: ©marilyna; page 4: ©Kicky_princess; page 4 (apple): ©James Tillinghast; page 5: ©quatte; page 6: ©alexgrichenko; page 7: ©Mikhail Strogalev; pages 8-9: ©Betty Shelton; page 9: ©prasom99; page 10: ©BorutTRDINA; page 11: ©glennimage; page 12: ©NinooN; page 13: ©CasarsaGuru; page 14: ©cherrybeans; page 15: ©HarryCollins; pages 16-17: ©Rebecca Bloom Chapman; page 17: ©4FR; page 18: ©MinShi; page 19 (map): ©pop_iop; page 19a: ©miwa_in_oz; page 19b: ©Nearchos; page 19(c): ©phototrip; page 20: ©milehightraveler

Edited by: Kim Thompson
Cover and interior design by: Rhea Magaro-Wallace

Library of Congress PCN Data

Pollination Pals / Jodie Mangor
 (Super Science)
  ISBN 978-1-73161-435-3 (hard cover)
  ISBN 978-1-73161-230-4 (soft cover)
  ISBN 978-1-73161-540-4 (e-Book)
  ISBN 978-1-73161-645-6 (ePub)
Library of Congress Control Number: 2019932077

Rourke Educational Media
Printed in the United States of America
01-3382311937